Improve Your Writing Skills

Powerful Techniques toward Mastering Writing

By Cathy Wilson
Copyright © 2014

Income Disclaimer

This book contains business strategies, marketing methods and other business advice that, regardless of my own results and experience, may not produce the same results (or any results) for you. I make absolutely no guarantee, expressed or implied, that by following the advice below you will make any money or improve current profits, as there are several factors and variables that come into play regarding any given business.

Primarily, results will depend on the nature of the product or business model, the conditions of the marketplace, the experience of the individual, and situations and elements that are beyond your control.

As with any business endeavor, you assume all risk related to investment and money based on your own discretion and at your own potential expense.

Liability Disclaimer

By reading this book, you assume all risks associated with using the advice given below, with a full understanding that you, solely, are responsible for anything that may occur as a result of putting this information into action in any way, and regardless of your interpretation of the advice.

You further agree that our company cannot be held responsible in any way for the success or failure of your business as a result of the information presented in this book. It is your responsibility to conduct your own due diligence regarding the safe and successful operation of your business if you intend to apply any of our information in any way to your business operations.

Terms of Use

You are given a non-transferable, "personal use" license to this book. You cannot distribute it or share it with other individuals.

Also, there are no resale rights or private label rights granted when purchasing this book. In other words, it's for your own personal use only.

Improve Your Writing Skills

Powerful Techniques toward Mastering Writing

By Cathy Wilson

Table of Contents

Introduction 9
Shot Gun Info on Writing Themes 11
Do You Have, Want, or Even Need a Particular
Writing Style? 19
Tips to Make the Most of Your Writing Time.........25
Obstacles WILL Appear – Tips to Battle Writing
Interference and Win! 31
Five Action Steps to Improve Writing Content........37
Strategies to Handle Rejection 41
Top Secret Tips to Make Money Writing – Even if you
Suck! 47
Writing Blunders Straightened Out.......................53
Final Thoughts 57

Introduction

A very dumbass man once told me that, "Everyone has the gift to write inside them!" He said it convincingly, with enthusiasm, while sporting beer-goggles and somehow half of a very odd smile.

THE TRUTH???

I'll give credit where credit is due. This "man," and I'm being prim proper polite here, was *sort of* correct here, technically speaking anyway. Mr. Dumbass was correct in the sense that I'm sure pretty much every living being with a few years under their belt has the ability to write at least something, which of course is futile in the hugely competitive world of writing, particularly e-book writing. It's our directional focus.

I doubt you've got much use for a doctor that "kinda" knows how to diagnose and treat a broken clavicle, particularly if you've just busted yours up! Point made.
I have been given the gift of writing and currently reside in about my 20th year of seriously perfecting my skills. I have done all "blood, sweat and tears" stuff for you and

now am passing along my expert introductory based knowledge to you, delivered in a polite, sweet and extremely caring manner.

The clear-cut purpose of this guide is to help you take whatever writing knowledge you have, and better it. Don't expect it to immediately turn to into a best-selling author. And don't you dare to expect it to be PERFECT!
You aren't perfect, I'm not perfect. The best I can do for you is to provide the best top quality practical information you can use to help improve your writing, delivering it in an engaging, easy to understand and "take action" manner and served up nicely for you to naturally absorb and utilize however you see fit.

Fair enough?
Now let me start releasing my thoughts before my head explodes and makes a gynormous mess!

Shot Gun Info on Writing Themes

Let's dive right in here. It's important you have at least an introductory understanding of the different types, forms, themes, or whatever you'd like to call it, of writing. Why? Well, this tells you better what the author is trying to communicate to you how they are going to go about doing it. Use these "themes" to better fit into the molded **expectations** of your readers, which of course is going to set you up to look like a million bucks, well, your writing anyway.

On the technical side of writing, there are four main themes of writing. I've feel this needs to be expanded further, particularly for newbies. So I've included a few subcategories that will help you move one step closer to defining first off, what "type" of writer you really are or dream of becoming.

Basic Themes
Expository – This one could be exactly what I'm doing right now? Not quite. It's where the author aims to educate, describe or define the subject to the audience. This theme is highest in popularity, often exemplified in textbooks or research and academic books.

This writing delivery is formal, like wearing a tux to a wedding. There isn't any personal opinion on it, rather it's just plain old boring facts. Sorry. I shouldn't taint your brain with that. It just brings to mind all those boring history books I painful read in my younger years.

This writing is not subjective and "How-to" online articles are a great practical example. And just so you know, when it comes to the "tux" thing, a sexy string bikini is more my "theme."

Narrative – Now, we're moving into the good stuff. Narrative writing is used when you're creating a biography, novel or perhaps testing the waters with heartfelt romantic poetry. It's where you are telling a story and hopefully, your audience is emotionally attached to your words hook, line and sinker.

It's where the author, that's you, skillfully puts themselves in the shoes of the character and reflects. Included are deliciously devilish plots and subplots, unique and interesting characters that just magnetically draw you in and demand you form an opinion, a love or hate relationship in the flesh.

With this narrative theme people get excited because they are given the tools to relate, actually envisioning themselves in the story themselves. Fiction is a perfect and straight to the point solid example.

Can you see me here?

Descriptive – This writing theme likely best describes my most successful theme of writing, although I tinker with each of them.

This sort of writing is all about setting your mind free and getting as descriptive as possible, making it a piece of cake for the reader to become interested, entertained and engaged in your writing. This triggers them to want to keep reading just because you are making them curious and you are offering up either an overdue escape from reality or great information that will help "better" them some way, somehow, whether it's physical, mental, social or emotional. As humans we are always looking to "feel" better.

Getting back to the "technical" side of writing themes, symbols, similes and metaphors are front and center here, and I know this is an introductory book. But if you aren't at least semi-familiar with those technical terms, I'm going to have to ask you to go back to Kindergarten and pay attention this time before you carry on reading.

Persuasive – If you're a "know-it-all" with a touch of narcissistic personality, you'll likely be pretty good at this theme. This writing is bias and often found in advertising and marketing campaigns. In high school you were probably asked to pick a side on a topic that's controversial and persuasively defend your beliefs. Ring a bell or two?

What you're doing is telling the reader the facts from the "right" angle, yours. You do know, Cathy Wilson's books are the most informational, masterfully written, engaging and entertaining books you can find online today. A perfect example!

Careful though. It's great to display how you feel about something but never forget there's two sides to every coin. And when you're finished it is only fair to be open to challenges, every once in a while someone's going to tear a strip or two off you. Just think of it as "conditioning" in your writing development plan.

BONUS THEME – Creative Writing – This theme of writing is extremely popular and I feel it warrants mention here. My book – my rules – like it or lump it! Croativo writing ic a very general terms that refers to a writing theme with the main focus of entertaining the reader, meaning the writing is typically engaging, flowing and perhaps off the beaten path. It's where a writer throws the rules of writing out the window and let's their fingers do the talking, directed of course by a free thinking and gynormously imaginative mind.

Sub-Themes
These kinds of writing are not headlining the show, but they are notably towards the front of the stage, where you might pay attention to one in particular simply because they're standing stark naked in front of you! Ha. Now pay attention. We're having a quiz at the end.

Random Thought – The best writing comes from a mind without interference, where a writer isn't afraid to let the thoughts popping into their mind, seeping onto the pages, of course depending on the audience there are times when you have to hinder these thoughts at little. At least I do. Or I could really get myself into a whole whack of trouble.

Point is, don't be afraid to test the waters here. Let your guard down and don't worry so much about what others might think of you. Rather let your mind, gut, expert knowledge and fingers sing. You've gotta start somewhere right?

Before moving on I'd like to be clear that each of the following fits into the main "themes" of writing. The last thing I want to do is rustle up confusion when teaching the ABC's of writing.

Business – This theme finds itself often in the workplace. It's a form of expository writing where facts are needed to effectively progress. In other words the purpose is to "take action."

Argumentative – Gotta love this one! This one is great when trying to naturally push someone's buttons. I remember writing an article on *helium* about my opinion of abortion, saying that men had no right when it came down to the final call simply because it wasn't their body. It's not right or wrong, just a fact. Wow. Talk about learning to defend myself. I felt like a chicken with two broken legs locked in a barn with 100 stray and very hungry cats! The idea here is to try and convince the reader your thoughts are right. And we all want to be right, right? *Informational* – Prim and oh so proper comes to mind here. A writing type or theme whereby the author, that's you, delivers information for that very purpose, to enlighten the reader in a not necessarily engaging way, clearly and concisely about the topic at hand.

Contrast and Comparison – This one's pretty straight forward. It's another example of expository writing where the author takes a topic or idea and shows what's similar and different. It's just like taking a square and a circle and describing the things alike and not. You should be a pro at this one if made that first big step graduating from kindergarten!

Expressive or Emotional – This sub-theme often gets me into trouble because I carry this one into writing projects that aren't supposed to have any personality or subjectivity to them whatsoever. Oops!

This is my favorite creative writing. It's where you get to open your imagination and let all your crazy uninhibited purely virgin thoughts, feelings and perspective flow.

This is REAL writing to me, letting someone in, get be-
dazzled with just how your weirdo mind works. The
thought makes me smile.

Poetry – Here you've got imaginative or "visual" writing,
the author reflecting and communicating to you in such a
way that you can relate much deeper than words. Poetry
usual has emotional meaning to the author which is re-
flective in the way they write, with the full intentions of
tapping into your emotions, carrying you along with them
through their journey.

Literary Reply – Simply put, this is where you reflect what
you think about a specific piece of writing. It could be the
review of a book or thesis paper. It's often constructive
and critical, used to make a literary piece better, or perhaps to persuade people as to why they should buy it. It's
expository writing through and through.

Biographical Narrative – Here, you'd share a heartfelt
personal experience with the author from your perspective, of course not right or wrong, subjective and geared
towards helping the audience understand and relate better, in most cases at least.

Technical – Another "boring" form of writing to me. Sorry.
Information is delivered without delay. Straight forward, to
the point, in a technical informational manner. Another
expository all the way.

Reactive – This sub-theme of writing is expected and
triggered. The responses to someone's opinion, views or
theory. It's a viewpoint, subjective in nature and falls under the expository theme.

Process/Stages – You might you this sub-theme in a
chemistry experiment. Explaining to the reader the pro-

cess in which something unfolds. Think step one, step two etc. here and you're on the right track. I'm not going to expand further here because chemistry was not one of my strong suits in school for sure.

Research – Another more "sciencey" sub-theme. Writing that's expository with the purpose of researching and re-porting new knowledge gained.

Educational – Here you are writing for the purpose of teaching in the academic sense. So you might be creat-ing worksheets for a grade 3 curriculum with the Simcoe County Board of Education. It's matter-of-fact expository writing at its best.

Angled – This one is extremely versatile, where you take any theme of writing and twist it the other way, reflecting on it from another angled expected or otherwise. It's a loose term that fits with any theme of writing. If you think about it this sub-theme, it could make an expository piece of writing creative. Or does that just mess you up?
Of course with these sub-themes you can make up ten zillion if you had all the time in the world. I've brought to your attention the most popular themes and sub-themes you'll need to at least have an overview of if serious about become tops with your writing.

My Thoughts…
This is where it can get scary because I'm supposed to effectively communicate to you the thoughts running through my brain in a mesmerizing, entertaining and in-formative manner! How am I doing so far?
The point here is by better understanding themes or types of writing, you will have the main tool you need to find the purpose and fulfill it in whatever writing you do. It just makes sense that if you are writing the steps to a science experiment which should be precise, matter-of-

fact and military-like, that if you start throwing your crea-
tivity in or reflecting on it poetically, you're really going to
throw your prof into "No-Man's Land!" The thought is fun-
ny, but that's a move with cause for dismissal.
You're a smart cookie and I know you understand the
basics here. It's time to move on.

Do You Have, Want, or Even Need a Particular Writing Style?

Everybody has a different style. Your hair may be a bee-hive style. Your clothes might be super duper slick and sexy and your may prefer newness when it comes to buying a house rather than the old rustic "character" style. Not judging, just saying.

If you want to write and write well, to the point of being recognized and followed by eager beaver readers, then you've got to either have a "style" in your possession or create one. And by creating one I just mean keep on writing so that one will manifest in time, a style that is effective and that you enjoy or can learn to love.

THE POINT??
Well if your so-cool buddy happened to buzz his beautiful locks of hair in exchange for a mohawk, this would be the point, triggering you to do the same because as an impressionable youngster, "monkey-see-monkey-do." And you realized in time that style of hair just sucks.

Then of course, you would make a plan to grow it out and change your style, searching for that hairstyle you actually liked instead of something you "thought" you might be okay with.

The same thing goes with creating your writing style.
If you don't enjoy your writing style – it WILL show in your writing. Writing is emotion – never forget it.
"Writing Style" standing on its own is gynormously subjective. For me, I choose to keep it simple, basic and straight to the point. There's no room in an introductory writing book for causing unnecessary confusion.
Are you going to choose a style that's:

*Personal
*Interpersonal

With your style you're giving the reading the information required to relate. It's where you are "figured out" on the criteria of your:

*dictation
*tone
*rhythm
*voice
*figures of speech

It's a start anyway. It's your style that will give your writing depth and meaning, that magical draw that opens the mind of the reader to let your words in, so that you can effectively pass the chosen message along and find purpose in the words your write, whether it's books you're crafting, articles, technical papers, reports, poetry, short stories or reviews.

It's your style that's going to give you're the tools to sink or swim in the literary world.

A writing style must be authentic. It's can't be faked or fabricated. Personal or interpersonal is what it has to be.

Impersonal Style – This style is what I think of as educator or prissy. It's prim and proper and often used for government documents, scholar papers and other "official" writing.

It includes the writer's experiences, thoughts and feelings. Interconnected with external factors and treats them as such, instead of being affected by the reader's emotions or "feelings." Cold comes to mind here, not in a nasty sense but in a "bullet point facts" sense. That's it in a nutshell, anyway.

Personal Style – This is the one I love. Intimacy is involved, personal, direct and simple. The writer expresses themselves and their unique CHOSEN approach. Beliefs, dreams, fears and desires are unleashed. The reader is invited in with open arms to experience and reflect.

A journal, texting, social media messaging and e-mailing are all perfect examples. With me, it really doesn't matter what type of book I'm writing. My unique personal style is somewhere to be found. Sometimes it's right in your face. Other times, you've got to do a little digging.

Having a personal, still is the one CONTROLLABLE factor in writing that can make you hugely successful. A well-crafted style takes years and years to perfect. Even then, it still needs work.

Just don't ever stop fine-tuning your personal style. Trust me on this one.

Differences Between Impersonal and Personal?

The kind of writing you are choosing, often dictates the "style" of writing you need to pull out of your hat. Some believe the choice is absolute. I do not, even if you are writing something fact-only, official or otherwise. You can still have some "personal" in it, just not as much as you might normally when writing an article or short paper.

I view the style more in percentages than anything else, less personal and more impersonal with the technical writing, obviously more if not all personal with the creative stuff. You get what I mean here. Even on an interview questionnaire you can still have a little personal. But, of course I am the black sheep of the writing world at times.

Distinctive Technical Features in Either Writing Style
There are distinctive technical aspects to each writing style, for the most part anyway. They will help you identify what style of writing the author is choosing and you can figure out the "why?"

Some of which are:
*Active or Passive Voice – Impersonal uses passive and Personal uses active
*Contractions – Impersonal normally doesn't use contraction and Personal does
*Rhetorical Questions – These are considered allowed with Personal and not with Impersonal
*Sentence Length – Personal normally uses shorter sentences, whereas impersonal style comes with the expectancy of more length
*Sentence Subject – With Personal style come people as the subject and things match with impersonal
Okay, that's enough of that. This gives you the bare bones basics of understanding a little bit about style.

My Thoughts…
I can't stress how important style is in any sort of writing you do. It is the one tool you control that can set you apart from the rest. We're talking oceans apart in an upward fashion.
Commit to continuously develop and fine-tune your chosen writing style, or rather the style that chooses you. It's your leverage to bigger and better in the wild and crazy world of writing.

Tips to Make the Most of Your Writing Time

Time is money, right?
It's especially difficult for writer's working at home. Excuses to do anything but write are everywhere around you. There's cleaning to be done, bills that need to be paid, kids that need feeding. The list goes on forever and ever amen!

Here are a few strategies that will help you make writing a priority and still get everything else done, by maximizing the effectiveness of your writing and minimize the crap that interferes with you just getting it done!

Create a Plan!
This is a must and needs to be completed BEFORE you begin your day. My suggestion is you either write your plan for the week, or in the least, before your head hits the pillow, jot down a timeline to get your writing done the next day.

*Hold Yourself Accountable! – By setting specific times to write. And by actually writing down what "part" of writing you're going to take with each time. You're going to get your writing done and feel productive and alive too.

FACT...
Anybody in life that's successful has a plan. Actually they probably have more than one. A short term and longer term one for sure. Add to that a plan for each day separately too. Planning is productive and the sooner you get used to that, the quicker you're going to stop procrastination and get crazy-nuts successful in your writing.

Control Social Interruptions
This one never used to matter. Today though, it's front and center stage for the one thing that can kill a writing career. It's a bit drastic, I know, but oh so true.

If you let your texting, facebooking, pinning and other neat phone features control you, they will. How many times have you set out to return a text or email and ended up screwing an hour of your day away fiddle faddling around? One thing leads to the next and all that adds up to in NOTHING getting done.

Take control here.
A magnificent strategy is to POWER OFF your device while you are writing, even if it's just for a few hours at a time. This gives you uninterrupted time to write. And don't worry, all your messages are still going to be there when you turn your device back on.

Just get set for a heck of a lot of "bing-ding-tingles" for the first while anyway. It may send your heart racing, but it IS necessary if you're serious about getting your writing done.

Take Breaks
Try not to be an "all or nothing" here. Making sure regular breathers are in your writing routine will help you become a more effective and efficient writer. If you're not recharging throughout your day there are unnecessary consequences:

*Your butt might fall asleep from sitting too long
*Your thinking will start to clutter
*You could become less effective because you're not as sharp as you were FIVE hours ago
*Perhaps you're hungry and not concentrating
*You may even start crying and that's not a good thing because physiologically logic and emotion just don't mix well.
*Distractions happen easier when solitarily confined for long periods of time
It happens even if it's just for 5 or 10 minutes. Make sure you stand up and get a breath of fresh air every hour or two. It will do you great mind, body and soul.

Set Yourself up for Success
What I mean here is you must consider your preferences and tolerances. If you're a morning person then perhaps that's when you should be scheduling most of your writing time? Figure out a way to do it.

If your clock has always screamed then you might better have been born an owl. Then set your schedule up so you can write during the wee hours of the morning. It doesn't matter whether or not it makes sense to anyone else. It needs to make sense to you if it's going to work. Don't think about this one too long.

Use Technology to Make Life Easier
It really doesn't matter what "era" you're from. The internet technology at your fingertips today makes it crazy-

nuts easy to get yourself organized and productive. There are all sorts of "schedulers" on-line that will hold you accountable to your time line in which to write your masterpieces!

Google and Microsoft are only the beginning here. What you need to do is take the time to figure out which programs appeal to you and start utilizing them.

For me, I pretty much just schedule everything into my iphone. For really important pointers, I actually set them up as reminders so that I've no excuses for not taking the time to just get it done. Often I'll schedule these a few times, just in case I happen to have my phone set on mute!

Why wouldn't you want to make it easier to make your time more productive? These are my thoughts exactly.

Reward Yourself – You Deserve it!
Remember as a child how much you looked forward to "treats?" Whether it was a bag of candy at the end of a good week of school, or a new laptop for getting honors on your report card, it doesn't matter what the reward is. What matters, is the fact you knew you were getting one for doing a great job. Recognition is something we so easily seem to give, but often forget we deserve it too, a tool to drive you forward positively. It's an incentive and concrete motivational tool that's going inspire you to want more and ultimately achieve each goal faster.

What sort of rewards should you give yourself?
*If you love shoes. Why not treat yourself to a pair after a particularly challenging goal is complete?
*Perhaps you've finally published your first non-fiction health and wellness book! Treat yourself to a nice dinner

out instead of the pre-packaged food you've been living on while slaving away with your book.

*If you love nature. Why not set aside extra time on the weekend to go for a nice relaxing hike. Maybe you want to set a whole day aside to explore the zoo. If it makes you smile, then you deserve to do it.

*Maybe you LOVE traveling and just haven't made the time to do so because you've been so busy with your writing? No worries. It's time for you to get the most of both worlds. Set a time frame to get a certain amount of writing complete, after which you are going to put on a blindfold and wildly throw a dart at a map. Wherever it lands is where you're going to be destined for a reasonable amount of time.

So maybe you'll work madly for 6 weeks and then jet off to majestic Belize? You can visit me there if you aren't leaving before September 2014. It's where I'm relocating! My point is, I want to remind you just how important it is to intermittently reward yourself. Don't' think about it – just DO IT!

My Thoughts…
Taking a "break" from writing is only going to inspire you positively. Cleansing your mind and moving you forward faster than a snail's pace. If you want to soar it's important for you to take the "time" you need to make it happen. Take your breaks. Schedule your breaks so you can "make it happen."

Obstacles WILL Appear – Tips to Battle Writing Interference and Win!

It doesn't really matter what genre of writing you're doing. At one time or another you will hit a brick wall with your writing and it will be frustrating. It's important you understand this and have to tools or rather mindset to deal with them. Trust me on this one. They're going to smack you right side the head when you least expect it.

You never set out en route to your destination expecting to get into a car accident to you? It just happens. It's the same thing with writing obstacles. They knock on your door out of the blue and don't normally go away if you slam the door in there face.

Here are a few common issues or obstacles writers face and the solutions to bust right through these walls and reach your writing goals without a scratch:

*Time Pressures – In this fast paced world of ours, time never seems to be on our side. There are only so many hours in the day to pack everything in, eating, sleeping, errands, kid's soccer and hockey, friend time, relaxation, and so forth.

If you don't commit to setting aside and scheduling the time to write, it just won't get done. Bite off pieces you can chew or your liable to choke and get nothing done.

The Solution
For example: If you need ten hours to finish up your manuscript and you've got four days to get it done. Start right away and schedule the majority of this writing time into the first few days. This means you're going to take the pressures off YOU to get it done. Just knowing you've a few extra days if some dire emergency arises is enough to keep this "dire emergency" away.
Mind over matter here.

So get two hours done in the morning and evening for the first two days, and you'll cruise through to the finish line. Set yourself up for success and ALWAYS opt for sooner not later, particularly when you have a writing project that has strict deadlines. An overly stressed and pressured writer is NOT a good writer.

Work hard, but manage your time wisely. Be reasonable and understand you are human and "shit" happens. Relax and write. Keep doing that and you're on your way straight to the top!

*Infamous Writers Block – Now this is the most over-used excuse I have ever heard. You're probably not going to believe this. But I have *"averaging"* over 5,000 words a day religiously for over 3 years now. Never once have I experienced writer's block.
Why?

Well, if the thoughts I want are flowing freely in my head. I just flip the angle, open another door and they always come busting through. It helps that I always have more than one project on the go. So when a particular topic just isn't working for me, I just switch gears and dive into another one.

My true belief?
Writers block is a figment of YOUR imagination. Sorry, but it's true. It's your mind telling you that you really don't want to write, going so far as to block your mind from doing so. To me, this just means the intrinsic communication between your wants/needs/desires and your brain, just aren't open enough. Not good or bad, just is.

The Solution
May I suggest two different approaches?
The first, is to bear down and push through this minor frustration. Keep writing and your "writers block" will pass. It has to at some point. It's always good to build you backbone a little anyway. Keep at it and it will go away.

The next, just switch gears. Always have a couple projects you are writing simultaneously. Often, for unconscious reasons, you will be better at writing one project versus another. Trust your instincts on this and give your mind the option. It can't hurt, right?
Nobody likes to be corners. This goes for your noggin too.

Social Disuassion – I hate to admit it, but writers often get a bad rap. Society is still way behind the times in understanding that writers don't have to be starving artists for life. Writing careers can be hugely successful and incredibly lucrative.

Stick with your guns here and don't make excuses to write. You deserve to write because you want to and don't need any reasons to do it.

The other side of the coin here is the fear your writing will be rejected because you're opening up your vulnerabilities and writing things that get emotions involved. It's tough to overcome this fear because we are intrinsically programmed to "care" what others think. Humans need each other and this means right or wrong, we need and want to "fit in." Often, so badly we will shape or thoughts, actions and believes in order to do just that.

The Solution
Stick to your guns here. What you are feeling and thinking deserves to be heard and don't let any social fears persuade you otherwise. Don't think about it here, just go for it. The best writing begins with a ridiculously true and open mind. From there you will open the doors of opportunity. Trust in this and you're headed in the "right" direction for you.

*Uninspired – Don't make such a big deal about this one. Everyone feels uninspired or de-motivated from time to time. My suggestion is to just push on through and search for whatever it takes to get you re-inspired.

The Solution
My mindset is to just coast a little when this happens, just as long as you don't stop writing the moment will pass. This is very difficult to do, but when you master this you are only going to strengthen your writing.

If you think of it like you would working out, there will be days when you're finding it hard to focus, where you're just going through the motions and have a hard time jet getting through your workout. All you need to do here is just make it through. Then, when you get to the next time when you're just flying through your workout on cloud ten, you're realize that "off" day was necessary for this "spectacular" day to happen.

The same thing applies with writing.
Just keep at it and you will naturally inspire yourself. If you truly love to write, this WILL happen. Believe it.

*Health Issues – I've added this one because so many people use health problems or issues as an excuse. I've "been-there-done-that" and am living proof excuses just suck. I still found a way to write after being hit by a ¾ ton truck, fighting for my life with the stress worrying about my little ones at home not sure whether or not I was going to make it. That thought in itself, nearly did me in. But guess what? Obviously it was not at the capacity I was used to. I *still* found a way to write. A lot of it was for personal reasons, but that's beside the point.

There are ZERO excuses on the face of this earth, universe and beyond you can tell me that make it impossible for you to write nothing at all.
So go ahead and try if you want. You'll just be unproductive and totally full of hot air.

The Solution
It's all about committing to write or not, no matter what the health issues you are dealing with, whether they are unexpected or chronic. You have a choice. You can CHOOSE to find a way to write, or you can CHOOSE to run through the list of excuses until you find the one you want to trick yourself with.
I'll leave that one with you.

My Thoughts…

If you can't tell already, I'm not one that handles excuses well. If you are looking to make excuses you'll find them and the consequence in lack of productivity. It's a choice to SEARCH for obstacles that can justify your lazy-ass actions. Sorry, but you know and I know it's the truth!
I understand it's important to recognize obstacles that are attempting to veer you off course. That I get. Just understand you are calling the shots and it's YOU that gets to decide if you're going to pick out a "one-size-fits-all" excuse or not.

Five Action Steps to Improve Writing Content

There are literally hundreds of action steps you can take to improve your writing. This book is an introductory book and hence I've simplified it quite extensively. Here are five VIP factors in writing you just can't ignore, not if you've got what it takes to be successful with your words. How to I know? Let's just say I live, breathe and even eat writing! I have more articles, books, technical papers etc. under my belt that most writers accomplish in a lifetime. My logical brain would tell me there's gotta be something in here for you to gain?

Commit to Writing
Your first step to sharpening your writing skills is to seriously COMMIT to writing. We're not talking relationship commitment here. That might well send many of you heading for the hills.

What I'm referring to here is having or developing the mindset to write and program that is an absolute. It may

take time, but if you're not serious about your writing to start. How can you possibly expect to improve?
Well, you can't.

This one's up to you. Find it in yourself to commit to your writing and the continuous improvement of it and you WILL get better. It's not a matter of "if" at this point, but rather "when."

Get Organized
Unorganized equates to cluttered and chaos. Just think about the feeling you get when walking into a kid's messy room. Overwhelming, isn't it? Just the sheer thought of all that unorganized clutter is enough to send you to the looney-bin!

Make the choice to get organized in both your writing schedule and your writing workspace and you're ahead of the game, making it easier for you to get down and dirty with your writing when the time arises, instead of spending wasted hours clearing off your desk and trying desperately to find a space to unleash you deep dark secrets.

You get where I'm going from here. If you don't, then I guess you've still got your head stuck in the sand. Pull it out, shake the sand out of your ears and get yourself organized to write. Don't forget to vacuum up that sand though. The first step in making sure your organization sticks!

Learn the Technical
I will admit I'm not so keen about the technical of writing. But, I understand enough to know it needs to be addressed. Plus, I've had my ass kicked many times by clients of which I've been writing technical papers for, talk

38

about learning quickly how to sharpen my writing up ra-
zor sharp, and fast!

It's important to always have an open mind to improving
the technical of your writing. It doesn't matter whether
you're writing children's, non-fiction, fiction or otherwise.
The better you are technically, the better the finished
product.

Know your Audience
Just about before you do anything, you need to scope out
your target audience. Knowing this is going to help you
know what tone you should be writing in, not to mention
the technicality and vocabulary in your writing.
Writing a paper that's got a grade 7 vocabulary and an
academic tone isn't going to fair well if you're writing a
children's book, an extreme example I know, but necessary to make my point.

Research your target audience and ensure you're writing
will fulfill expectations and more importantly be under-
stood. If you don't, you might as well just be writing for
fun because it will fall upon deaf ears.

Practice Fine-Tuning
This pointer calls for your mind to be WIDE open in anything you do. If you aren't always consciously open to
strengthening your skills, it's just not going to happen.
With writing, it's all about taking the time to find ways to
make your writing better.

This is true whether it's reading up on finding ways to improve the flow of your writing, or even just working on
your vocabulary or unique writing style. Even trying different genres of writing from time to time is all good.

The point here is that you need to always look for way so to fine-tune your craft because that's what serious and successful writers do.

CHOOSE to work at perfecting your writing skills and you'll do just that.

My Thoughts...
I guess we'd better stop there cuz we've already hit five! As mentioned, there are oodles of tips, tricks and strategies you can use to continuously better your writing.
NEWSFLASH!
There is no quick route here. You either do the time and get results, or you don't.
For the ten millionth time, here it's YOUR choice.

Strategies to Handle Rejection

Here we're going to look at this from a psychological perspective. That is what drives all that you write, theoretically anyway. And understanding it further will only mean happier and more productive writing days for you!

It's not something most look forward to in life. But rejection and failing are a fact of life. You only learn here by doing. And when it comes to handling rejection you've just got to go through it to learn your best coping mechanisms.

There is risk in everything you do. Some of it is controllable and some is not, when you are searching for acceptance or approval from others you are risking rejection. When you write you are putting yourself "out there" each and every time.

Perhaps you wrote a phenomenal book last month that made your proud. However, last week you got blasted with some "tough to swallow" reviews that caused questions as to your skills as a writer, comments so harsh that if you were truly a wimp. It would have sent you with your tail wagging between your legs and into a quiet dark solitary corner to just exist.

But you're not, so you needn't worry on that one!
Overly sensitive people have a tough time dealing with rejection. That's okay. What you need to do is learn your preference and tolerance level and be ready to act accordingly.

Instances aside from your writing where rejection is often center stage are:

*Boyfriend or girlfriend in school
*Applying for a job
*Trying to get in with a particular social circle
*College or university application
*Trying to seek the approval of a boyfriend's family
*Trying to launch a new business plan
*Testing out a new meal for dinner
*Taking your family to a new restaurant
*Vacationing somewhere new
The list here goes on infamously.

It really doesn't matter if you are Mr. or Mrs. Confidence in the flesh. Inevitably, you will face rejection and it's normal to question yourself and beliefs when this happens.

What matters here is how you deal with rejection, your mindset, and how it affects your actions immediate and your life direction. You're continuously making decisions and if you don't handle rejection well, this can negatively impact you and your writing in this instance, perhaps more than it should.

Here are a few tips, tricks or trains of thought that will help you deal with and overcome rejection in writing. Again the only way to truly learn your best route is by doing. This will help get you started...

Understand Your Odds
This isn't about pre-judging or getting obsessed with the chances of you succeeding with any one book or writing project. Rather, it's about being honest with yourself and your writing abilities on each particular quest, a mindset that shouldn't be ignored.

If this is your first non-fiction book up for sale, don't expect it to be received with open arms by your readers, all your reviews stellar and not a negative comment in sight.

THE TRUTH?
Newbies have it particularly hard in the big bad world of writing. You need to "prove" yourself and your writing skills before people are willing to openly support you. Get ready to do this and understand fully "with your mind," that it will take time to work your way into the "good" books here.

Let some of the negative criticisms slide and learn from each. Flip them to positive. Learn to bite your tongue when necessary without making a fuss over it and you'll do just fine.

Talk yourself into understanding the odds of rejection and you will have a better more open mind to except whatever life throws at you.

Do NOT Keep ALL Your Eggs In One Basket!
I happened to grow up on a dairy farm and learned the hard way not to keep all me "hard earned" egg collecting in one basket ever again. I went out to collect the eggs

43

like I did every other morning. Carefully reaching into each of the hiding places my chickens laid they're eggs. I'd put each of the brownish speckled eggs into my woven brown basket.

Well, I was in a rush one morning and tripped on my gravel lane, running full tilt to the house. You guessed it. Smash went the eggs and instead of having fifteen or sixteen eggs, I had about three intact when I took inventory. My point?

Apply this hard earned lesson to your writing endeavors, whether you are submitting you manuscript to more than one editor or submitting a few different articles for consideration in magazine publications. The rejection pill is a heck of a lot easier to swallow when you *know* you've got other writing pieces being considered that very moment. Think of it as psychosomatic appeasement. If your head is happy – then you're going to be happier too.

With writing, it's critical to keep your momentum going. Hitting a brick wall is never fun. But it's not so bad when you know your truck's still running.

Keep in Mind Persistence Pays Off
Sure rejection isn't fun. In retrospect though, it means you're one step close to reaching your goal. Many world famous writers have had their work rejected numerous times. They *believed* in what they wrote and never just let it go. Months and often years later it paid off and they hit the jackpot.

Dr. Seuss was rejected, along with *Agatha Christie* and *Zane Grey*, who was told "You have no business being a writer and should give up." Crazy nuts, but true!
Use these scenarios as inspiration to deal with rejection in a positive light, or at least semi-positive.

Don't Take it Personally

I get it. This isn't easy because if you care about what you are writing, and someone else doesn't like it. You're going to take it smack off the front of your face. Try not to. Chances are pretty good that your writing was rejected for every other reason than "not being good enough." It could be that you don't have boobs. Maybe you remind the editorial staff of an annoying aunt. You caught the internal mail yahoo on a bad day. He doesn't like the color of the envelope you used and tosses it straight in the garbage. You're "rejected" without anybody reading it.

Even if you have someone calling you and telling you that you're writing just doesn't cut it, they may be passing the message along and still nobody may have even took the time to read it. Sad, but true.

Understand here that if you believe in yourself and your writing. You WILL get it published. Keep working on it and most importantly never give up.

My Thoughts…
You just can't bubble wrap yourself here. The sooner you accept and understand rejection, the better. ALL writers, famous or not, have been rejected at some point. And they're still rejected today. You just can't please everyone or that one particular person making the decisions for THEIR reasons.

Just commit to keep on writing and use the above pointers to help soften your landing. And you'll do just fine. Trust me on this one.

Top Secret Tips to Make Money Writing – Even if you Suck!

Unless you get very lucky, fall into the 1 in 100,000 category, and write a best seller right off the hop, you're going to have to play your cards right to make money writing. The truth is, writing is a tough career in general to make a living at.

Now, chin up. Are you a lover or a fighter?
This doesn't mean you can't do it, because you most definitely can. My perspective here is that many people don't really put much into their writing and end up just throwing in the towel. This adds fuel to the fire and makes the odds of being successful in writing "harder" than they actually might be.

Freelance writing is the place where most writers learn to earn some pretty good money consistently, if you've got a great business sense and reasonable to good writing skills. Then you're pretty much off to the races.

For you, I have some top secret tips that are only going to inspire you to start rolling in the dough…

Top Secret #1

Article writing is likely the most diverse "kind" of writing. It's where the sky is the limit, particularly if you get in with a good solid publication, or have photography skills to add to your writing value. You're going to do well filling your pockets with some nice green stuff.

There are oodles of online sites where you can set up an account for free and sell yourself to prospective clients, like anything you've got to start from the ground up, often working for peanuts to start. Most of these online marketing sites like Elance and Odesk, are driven by reviews. If you satisfy your clients, you'll slowly but surely work yourself up in the ranks with more clients coming to you for your expert writing services AND you will have the ability to increase your rate accordingly and still get hired! The more specialized you are, the better. There's a demand for most any kind of writing from product descriptions and reviews to web content, technical papers, short stories, ebooks, essays and PRs to business plans and songwriting. You name it and it can be lucrative.

Personal Touch
I worked my way up out of the trenches of Elance, writing in the beginning for 16 plus hours a day for less than $3/hr. That's right. In my head, I categorized this as "experience." Well, it paid off and just shy of 2 years later I was able to comfortably ask up to $20/hr for any particular writing project. My account is still there, but I'm so busy with my book writing, I rarely check in. It's an amazing feeling, but a heck of a lot of work!

Bottom line is. If you stick with your writing and are at least half-decent, you can make some decent money. It just takes time!

Top Secret #2
Aim for the sun and if you reach the stars you'll be a happy camper! Think about your dream publication, what you love to write about and where it would be a dream come true to see it appear.
Not go out and get it!
Write your article or book and send it off to the publication. What have you got to lose? Absolutely nothing.
-You'll gain experience

-Get your foot in the door, or at least your toe
-It may take you years, but eventually if you keep persisting *somebody* is going to let you in!
-Practice handling rejection with no crazy-nuts expectations
With this sort of bold move, the pressure is off. Often when you take a shot in the dark in life you really do hit the bulls-eye. Try it. Your aim could be better than you think.

Top Secret #3
Find your crowd. What this means is, get off your lazy butt and get connected with fellow writers, editors, publishers and anyone else in the writing industry. Why? To learn and grow, open doors of opportunity.

Most cities have conferences happening left, right and center. There's all the social media platforms including twitter, facebook, google plus. You name it and there are writing groups with oodles for you to gain.

Immerse yourself here. Life, breathe and eat it and you are only going up with your writing endeavors. Just trust me on this one. If you want to make money writing you MUST continuously expand your knowledge base.

Top Secret #4
Ask around. Every single business you see around you, online, and anywhere else in this whole gynormous world of ours needs writing services to succeed. Many either just don't know it or they have lost focus and need you to redirect their attention to how badly they need your specialty writing services.

This one's a no-brainer. Get out of your big comfy lazy boy chair and start asking. The worst that can happen is you get told to bugger off. The best case scenario is you get the gig and nicely get to pad your wallet because of your straight forward guts!
Ask and you shall receive.

Top Secret #5
Just DO NOT stop! By stopping, you are selling yourself short. The more you write the better you get, and the closer you are to reaching your goals. When you quit, it's pretty much guaranteed that a few more days at it would have hit the jackpot. That's just how life works.
In e-book writing in particular there are so many different factors necessary to be successful, that it's downright overwhelming. Don't let this fact take you down. One foot in front of the other. Do what you can. And no matter what DO NOT STOP WRITING. If you aren't writing then you can't succeed. The rest will help you get there, but it's the expert book writing that's the "seed" here.

If you quit, there's obviously no way in beep you're going to make any money writing. If a baker quits coming in for his early morning shift baking bread, he's going to have to face the wrath of his wife coming home with no money in his holey pockets. Yikes!

Think like "Finding Nemo" and "Just keep swim-ming...Just keep swimming..."

My Thoughts...
The last thing I want to do here is overwhelm you or send you crying home to your mama. Read and understand these top secret writing tips to make money. Take what makes sense to you and apply. It's only going to help you achieve success sooner than you will on your own. Put that in your pipe and smoke it!

Writing Blunders Straightened Out

Myths and truths scatter pretty much anywhere on earth you venture to. When it comes to writing myths they really can be a pain in the butt, interfering with the route you're heading to reach your goals.

I know you're a pretty smart cookie. But here are a few false writing pointers that will lead you down the river to no water if you let them

Myth One – All authors are immediately famous.

Truth – Unless you just woke up this morning and decided to become a writer, chances are pretty good you know this one couldn't be more freakin false. The first clue? Publishing anything is a process that takes time. There's all the fine-tuning of the publication, the marketing and so forth. The list goes on and so will you. Right on past this myth and onto the next.

Myth Two – Get published and you're never going to see another rejection letter again!

Truth – What planet are you living on? Rejection has zilch to do with published. Many infamous published authors receive even more rejection afterwards. That's just the way the cookie crumbles. Rejection is a part of writing. Why not spin it this way? The more rejections you get the closer you are to making your mark on the literary world. Makes you smile, doesn't it?

Myth Three – A published book is a good book
Truth – Now this one is a big crock of crap! It would be nice if this was true, but it's not. Money talks, celebrity status talks. Social media supremacy talks more, if you have money or superb social status to buy "attention." You can get your thoughts down on paper and onto the book shelves. Sad, but true.

Pisses me off because even in the Children's book department I can write *Madonna* under the table! Unfortunately, I don't have the whole world bowing down to my feet to make this happen. Not *yet* anyway…lol
Just because a book is published, doesn't have anything to do with the quality of the contents. Another "sad, but true" moment.

Myth Four – After your first book is successfully published, every other book your write will follow in the "ace" suit.

Truth – If only it were that easy. It's not. YOU have to establish your credibility and market your talents as a writer continuously if you think more than one of your masterpieces will be published and flourish.
The Truth…

It really doesn't matter so much that your book is published. Is it selling copies should be your focus!

Myth Five – All writers are loaded.

Truth – Here's a loaded gun. There's no bullets in it so you can put it to your head and pull the trigger! Come on. In case you really have been hiding from reality, most writers do so on the side and never achieve higher than that.
What does that tell me?
There are writers out there that make it big and that's all I need to know.

Myth Six – After seeing your first cover it will lose its "wow" factor.

Truth – Maybe I'm just a mental case here. But every single time I see a cover of mine go up I get very happy rainbow butterflies dancing around in my tummy. TMI I know…but true!

Myth Seven – Your readers will always stand by your writing.

Truth – Huh? What world are you living in here? The truth is YOUR writers will be the first to stab you in the back. Actually they will go one step further as to LOOK for ways to take you down. Anything and everything you do that isn't absolutely perfect they will make sure you're aware of. Need I say more?

Final Thoughts

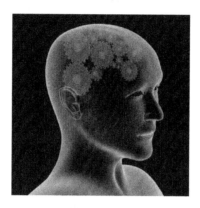

A writer is definitely a different kind of breed, or so I'm told anyway. And a truly gifted writer doesn't look for perfection. That just interferes with the unique thoughts, feelings and storylines seeking to escape from your brain. You don't want to taint these virgin thoughts with logic now, do you?

What's important is to trust yourself and your writing abilities enough to let the thoughts flow freely, from your mind directly onto the page as they fall. Let the editor worry about making them "literarily correct" for some of the nit-pickers that aren't really interested in your talents and what you have to say, rather they are looking for a way to justify how crappy they feel about themselves. Finding avenues to trash your heart and soul is fun and games for them!

With my introductory book you now have the tools in a basic sense for the technical. I hate to say if you don't at least get a B- in the techno of writing, you're likely going to fail come time for the big exam. Go back through my masterpiece in basics one more time if need be, then you should be good to go in that department, the base solid enough for more than one person to step on and not fall through!

In summary, here are some of the pointers we've discussed that are going to help you soar past the moon at lightning speed with your writing…

*Understand the technical basics, grammar etc.
*Find your expertise and exploit it!
*Whatever theme you're writing under, make sure you research and use credible niches
*Never underestimate the wide array of avenues in which you can make your writing talents lucrative
*Create a daily writing plan that works for you and stick with it
*A positive mindset is a must
*Don't ever quit!

Keep in your thoughts with every word you write you are perfecting your talents, and with every piece of writing your perfect you are one step closer to reaching your goals. It's mind over matter. Your belief WILL become your reality. I'm a perfect example that just keeps "going and going and going."

Take from my book what works for you and apply. If you've gained even just one pointer to help steer you in the direction of your writing vision, then I'm a very happy and ultimately successful writer!

In order for my books to rank and sell on Amazon they need positive reviews. If you enjoyed my book and have a few minutes to write a 3-5 line review about my book, that would really help me. Thank you :)

I hope that you enjoyed my book and you can check out all my other books by visiting my website at: flawlesscreativewriting.com

Disclaimer

CPSIA information can be obtained
at www.ICGtesting.com
Printed in the USA
LVOW13s1534300617

539951LV00010B/872/P